Lament for the holy city

Flute and piano

MUSIC DEPARTMENT

OXFORD
UNIVERSITY PRESS

OXFORD
UNIVERSITY PRESS

Great Clarendon Street, Oxford, OX2 6DP,
United Kingdom

Oxford University Press is a department of the University of Oxford.
It furthers the University's objective of excellence in research, scholarship,
and education by publishing worldwide. Oxford is a registered trade mark of
Oxford University Press in the UK and in certain other countries

ISBN 978-0-19-352374-6

Printed in Great Britain on acid-free paper by
Halstan & Co. Ltd, Amersham, Bucks.

Lament for the holy city
from *Visions*

This version of *Lament for the holy city*, for flute and piano, is an arrangement of an extract from John Rutter's *Visions*, which is scored for upper voices, solo violin, strings (or organ), and harp.

Available on sale or rental from Oxford University Press:

Visions vocal score (ISBN 978-0-19-351318-1)
Visions solo violin part (ISBN 978-0-19-351319-8)
Visions harp part (ISBN 978-0-19-351320-4)
Visions organ part (ISBN 978-0-19-351321-1)

Conductor's scores and string parts are available on rental only from the Oxford University Press Hire Library or appointed agent.

Visions has been recorded by Kerson Leong, the Temple Church Choristers, and Aurora Orchestra, conducted by John Rutter. The recording is on the Collegium label (COLCD 139).

Lament for the holy city is also available in its original scoring for violin and piano (ISBN 978-0-19-352308-1).

Lament for the holy city

JOHN RUTTER

Printed in Great Britain

OXFORD UNIVERSITY PRESS MUSIC DEPARTMENT, GREAT CLARENDON STREET, OXFORD OX2 6DP

John Rutter

Lament for the holy city

Flute part

MUSIC DEPARTMENT

OXFORD
UNIVERSITY PRESS

Lament for the holy city

JOHN RUTTER

OXFORD UNIVERSITY PRESS MUSIC DEPARTMENT, GREAT CLARENDON STREET, OXFORD OX2 6DP